malcolm cook

youth football

drills

age **7** to **11**

THIRD EDITION

Published by A & C Black Publishers Ltd
36 Soho Square, London W1D 3QY
www.acblack.com

Third edition 2009
Second edition 2004
First edition 1999
Reprinted 2001, 2003

ISBN 978 14081 0288 6

A CIP catalogue record for this book is available from the British Library.

Acknowledgements
Cover photograph © Getty Images.
Textual photographs © PA Photos.
Illustrations by Mark Silver.

Note: While every effort has been made to ensure that the content of this book is as technically accurate and as sound as possible, neither the authors nor the publishers can accept responsibility for any injury or loss sustained as a result of the use of this material.

A & C Black uses paper produced with elemental chlorine-free pulp, harvested from managed sustainable forests.

Typeset in 10 on 12pt DIN Regular
Printed and bound by Martins the Printers Ltd.

CONTENTS

ACKNOWLEDGEMENTS

I would like to thank Les Kershaw (Youth Consultant, Manchester United Football Club), who was instrumental in the development of the club's excellent youth scheme, for endorsing this book with his foreword. I would also like to thank Mark Silver for his excellent illustrations which bring the drills to life. Finally, best wishes to all the coaches who work with young players, wherever you are – your work makes a difference and is vitally important to the future of our great game – good coaching!

FOREWORD

Malcolm Cook's third book for the soccer market is timely with the advent of the Football Association Academies for the coaching and development of young soccer players. Very little literature on soccer has been dedicated to primary school children, who have tremendous enthusiasm and a capacity to learn new skills.

Anyone involved in developing young soccer players, from primary schools, junior clubs, Centres of Excellence through to Academies, will find this book useful. It gives a logical series of practices in all the basic techniques, without the need for specialised or expensive equipment. The practices are simple, but effective, and cater for all abilities. David Beckham, for example, gained exceptional skills in soccer by practising these kinds of techniques when he was a young player. His free kicks, crosses, and long and short passes are now acclaimed worldwide.

In *101 Youth Football Drills* Malcolm has successfully brought together his vast experience as a soccer coach and teacher in an easy-to-follow and practical manual. I recommend this book to both experienced and prospective coaches, and anyone with an interest in developing young soccer players.

Les Kershaw
Youth Consultant
Manchester United Football Club

INTRODUCTION

This book is designed to support the coach, teacher or parent, and aid them to obtain the best results from their practice sessions with young footballers. There are a number of books available on coaching methods and technical skill acquisition. However, the main aim of this book is to provide a comprehensive programme of varied, realistic and educationally sound drills for young players which will help them to improve progressively.

There is little attempt to tell the coach how to coach, for each one will employ his or her own unique style and characteristics that will, naturally, affect the learning of young players. I have noticed that some books containing drills are impractical and not designed for the particular age groups that are supposed to be using them. In this book I have attempted to provide the coach with a supply of practical and functional drills in a simple format which takes into account the growing needs of youngsters between the ages of 7 and 11 years. Young players at this stage are curious, enthusiastic and constantly on the go. They learn to become more co-ordinated over time, and the wise coach will allow them to experiment and play down the competitive element – they need plenty of variety as they learn new skills.

The players will learn to improve their skills, have fun and develop good social habits through the constant use of the drills. The role of the coach, teacher or parent is to provide the support, guidance and encouragement for young players to maximise their potential. I hope this book achieves what it sets out to do, and becomes a tried-and-tested tool kit of practical resource material for the coach in the years ahead.

It should be emphasised at the beginning that although we use the word 'he' throughout the book, this is only for convenience. It does, of course, also refer to female players, who give so much to the sport and are developing all the time in their own right.

Stephen Ireland, the Manchester City attacker, has shown much improvement this season. He has attributed this to increased practice – something that will work for all young players! (Photo: Mike Egerton)

PRACTICE ORGANISATION

The good coach will endeavour to produce an effective learning environment for his players that promotes safety, fun and purpose and ensures progression. He should plan each session beforehand and decide on the skills or topics that he wishes to help his players learn. He should select the combinations of drills from the book and arrive early at practice in order to set up and prepare equipment for the players. Good organisation generally makes for good coaching and motivation. Here are some basic guidelines for the coach to consider when using drills from the book.

practice service

The coach will have to demonstrate, and allow his players to practise ways of serving the ball to their team-mates. Some of the techniques will be familiar to them while some will be relatively new – however, all of them will be valuable to their learning. The majority of service actions are by hand as this tends to guarantee accuracy. However, as soon as the player can consistently kick the ball well then he can serve in this manner too.

These are the service techniques:

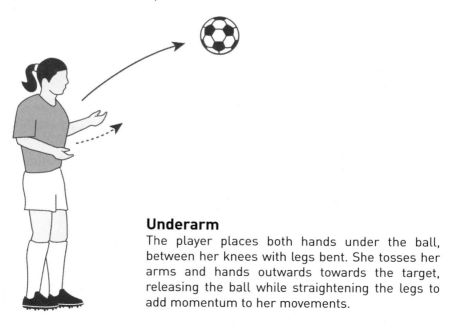

Underarm
The player places both hands under the ball, between her knees with legs bent. She tosses her arms and hands outwards towards the target, releasing the ball while straightening the legs to add momentum to her movements.

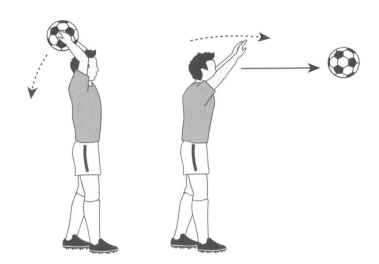

Throw-in The player places both hands around the back of the ball, which rests on the back of his neck. With one leg in front of the other to give himself a more balanced position, he bends his upper body backwards before swinging forwards in a smooth motion to thrust the arms forwards together and send the ball on its way.

Javelin The player balances the ball using one hand and wrist to secure it. The body is turned side-on with the other arm aiming towards the intended target. The player then whips his arm over and through to hurl the ball high and far.

Bowling (*see* top of page 13) The player holds the ball from below and crouches on one knee, swinging his arm backwards with the ball before swinging through to roll the ball along the ground.

Kicking Conventional techniques such as the push-pass (*see* figure middle left), using the inside part of the foot, are adequate for short-range services, while the instep-pass (*see* figure middle right) can be used to kick longer distances. If the service needs to be delivered higher, for example to give a player heading practice, then the player serving the ball can gently toss it up to himself before playing a volley-pass (*see* bottom figures).

Many of the drills require one of the players to serve the ball to a team-mate to allow him the opportunity to practise and develop his skills. As such, the delivery of the ball needs to be accurate, sensitive and realistic, whether the aim of the drill is to work on controlling, shooting or heading the ball. Remember the maxim: 'poor service starves the practice'.

footballs

Many of the drills do not require a lot of balls. However, where possible, the quality should be the best available, with particular attention paid to their size and weight. For example, when introducing heading to young players, make sure it is a 'pleasure not a pain' for them to practise by using a light ball. I find volleyballs are perfect at this stage until the players build up the necessary confidence and technique and can move on to the conventional football. It is a good policy for the coach to have a variety of balls of different sizes, colours, markings, weights and textures. He can then change them depending on the ages of the players, the skills being practised or the difficulty of the drill. Players will progress more quickly, develop greater sensitivity and 'touch' for the ball and generally be more motivated to practise with a variety of balls.

equipment

Self-discipline is part of being a good footballer. Build this quality in your players by getting them into the habit of assisting the coach to set up and take away equipment used in the practice session. Young players like to see an attractive learning environment where portable goals, coloured bibs and cones, varied balls and flag poles are safely set up – it's all part of the fun!

space

The distances and areas mentioned in the book are only approximate. The coach needs to observe how much space and time players require to make the practice drill effective. He should then modify it by having the players stand nearer or farther from each other, or enlarging or reducing the area they are working in. The space will depend on the players' sizes, maturity, ages and skill levels – don't be afraid to change distances when necessary.

The diagram on page 15, which shows one half of a junior-sized football field, could be utilised by using the flank areas A and B for crossing or long-kicking, while C could be used for goalkeeping, shooting or heading. Areas D and E could be used for small-sided games. The centre circle area F could be used for various skills or tactics.

The enterprising coach can also use cones on the ground to devise varied shapes such as squares, rectangles, circles and triangles for coaching purposes.

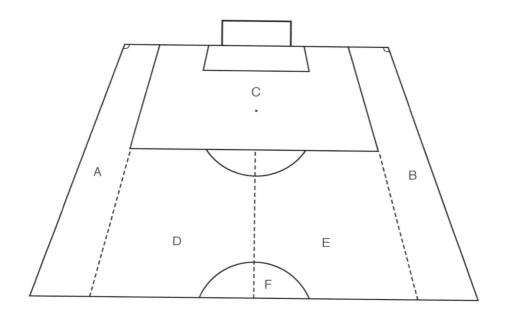

Another effective coaching aid is a wall. Indoor or outdoor, players can use garage doors, house walls or even boards. This is safer with a light sponge ball – no broken windows! The rebound surface can allow the player to attain many repetitions of practice in a short time.

numbers

Ensure that the number of players in each drill is relatively small so that every player has repeated opportunities to practise the skill and improve his ball control. There is nothing worse than having long files of bored youngsters awaiting their turn to perform skills – keep them active! However, the other extreme is for young players to work non-stop and become physically and mentally exhausted. The good coach will intersperse the more physically demanding drills with the lighter ones, in order to allow young players to work at their maximum without becoming overtired.

The drills can be used in a progressive way, working from the easiest to the more difficult. Alternatively, varied skills and drills can be used when the coach thinks fit. However, the same drill should not be used for too long as this can cause boredom. On the whole, youngsters have a shorter attention span than adults, so they do not like 'overcoaching' – it is best to repeat drills often but to keep them short.

Tottenham Hotspur's Luka Modric, shown here skipping past a tackle by Chelsea's Juliano Belletti, although having a slight physique, manages to compete against heavier opponents. A good warm up is essential for all players, no matter their physical condition. (Photo: Sang Tan)

WARMING UP

The coach needs to ensure that the players prepare themselves correctly – physically and mentally – before they commence practice. There are three main reasons why players should warm up.

1 To mobilise the joints of the body, increase blood flow, raise muscle temperature and stretch the muscles. This will allow the players to move through a greater range of movement and will help prevent injury.

2 To maximise performance. The body performs better when demand on the circulatory and respiratory systems increases gradually. Demanding physical activity will fatigue the body prematurely if the body is not warmed up.

3 To prepare mentally. The mind needs to 'tune-in' to the practice situation so, by rehearsing movement patterns from the game, the mind becomes activated and focused on the skills that are needed for practice.

The effective warm-up consists of three phases:

Phase 1 The first phase focuses on getting the whole body mobilised gradually. Light running activities are used to raise the body temperature and heart rate.

Phase 2 The second phase involves stretching the major muscles of the body and the joints. Particular attention should be paid to the specific muscles and joints that are used in playing the game, i.e. the spine, hips, and legs.

Phase 3 The third, and final, phase is the most intensive and involves activities performed at a faster tempo that allow players to practise and rehearse patterns of movements from the games. Note: players should do some light running after the stretches in phase 2 to raise the heart rate and temperature before starting this phase.

By the end of these three phases the players will be ready mentally and physically to get the best from the practice drills. Most coaches have enough material to carry out phases 1 and 2 competently, so the drills provided in this chapter are specifically designed for phase 3 of the warm-up.

Purpose: Sidestepping an opponent and changing direction

Practice set-up: Two files of players stand facing each other 10–20 yds apart with a cone placed in the centre. The first player from each file runs towards the other until they are 2–3 yds away. At this point they both dummy to go one way before changing direction and passing each other on the other side of the cone. The coach informs them which direction they should all take as they pass their partners. They then join the back of the other file and await their next turn.

Equipment: One cone or pole per group

Progressions: Players should practise dummying to both sides. As they progress, the tempo of the drill can be increased. Remember to indicate clearly what side the players should pass each other – we don't want a collision.

drill 2

Purpose: Marking and dodging movements

Practice set-up: Two files of players stand facing each other 10–20 yds apart in a channel and the players from each file work in pairs. The first player runs forwards towards the other side with his partner 'shadowing' him 1–2 yds behind. The leading player changes direction often, with his partner attempting to follow his every movement as closely as possible. As soon as they arrive at the other side, the next two players repeat the drill in the opposite direction. Each pair should alternate each time between being a 'leader' and 'shadower'.

Equipment: Four cones

Progressions: Start slowly and increase the pace as players improve.

Purpose: Changing direction and pace

Practice set-up: Two files of players face each other 15–20 yds apart in a channel 10 yds wide. The first player from one file runs across the area and tries to get across the far line to join the opposite file without the opposing player tagging him. Both players run towards each other and alternately attempt to evade, if they are an attacker, or close down, if they are a defender, their opponent. When they finish they join the file opposite and the next two players emerge.

Equipment: Four cones, one set of coloured bibs

Progressions: Make the channel narrower for the attacker or wider for the defender so that they have to be more agile in their running movements. Enforce a condition that the defender must come forward – this means no moving backwards or stopping.

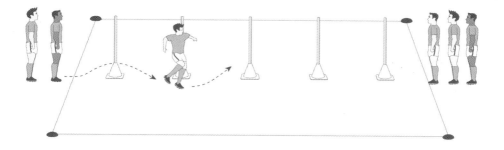

Purpose: Changing direction at speed

Practice set-up: Two files of players face each other 15–20 yds apart with a slalom of flag poles placed 1–2 yds apart on the ground. The first player runs in and out of the poles, ensuring that he does not touch them until he reaches the other side, where the next player repeats the exercise in the opposite direction.

Equipment: Six to eight flag poles

Progressions: To progress, the tempo can be increased, the number of poles can be increased, or the space between them narrowed to make it more difficult for the players to run through them. As the players improve, one player from each file can approach each other at the same time, making sure they avoid a collision. The players can practice continuously in this way.

drill 5

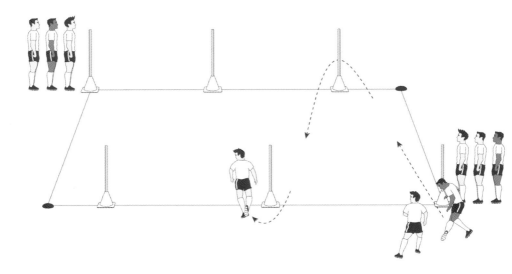

Purpose: To practise lateral movement

Practice set-up: Two files of players face each other 15–20 yds apart with a maze of flag poles placed on the ground 3–5 yds apart and adjacent to each other. The first player moves forwards and runs from one side to the other, moving through the maze until he reaches the other side, whereupon the next player sets off in the other direction.

Equipment: Six flag poles

Progressions: The tempo can be increased, or one player from each side can compete with an opponent to see which one can reach the other file first. If two players compete, they need to be careful that they avoid each other as they race. The movement pattern can be altered by each player skipping in a sideways direction, just like in a game.

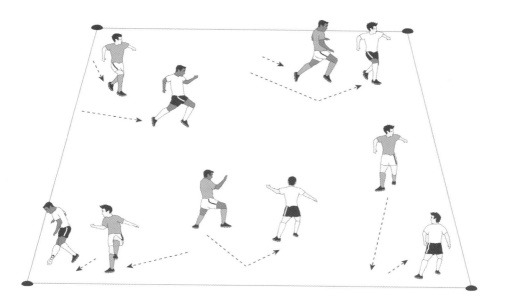

Purpose: Practice in stopping, starting, dodging, marking and changing direction at speed

Practice set-up: Players split up into pairs and work in a 10–20 yds square. Players are numbered 1 and 2 and one of them tries to escape the other who gives chase within the area. The player 'shadowing' the leading player does not actually touch him as they run; instead, he tries to keep as close to him as he can. The coach whistles regularly and all players must halt immediately when he does. If the 'chaser' can reach and touch his opponent, he gains a point; if not, the 'leader' gets the point. The chasers and leaders change roles after a set period.

Equipment: Four cones, two sets of coloured bibs

Progressions: After a set number of 'chases', the players count their points; to progress, the coach can change the pairs so that they work with other players.

drill 7

Purpose: General movement with changes of direction

Practice set-up: In an area 10–20 yds square, the players disperse and two players hold hands to form a 'chain' in the centre. The two players chase the others in the area and try to 'tag' them or force them outside the square. In either case, the tagged player joins the chain until one player is left. If the chain breaks at any time, then the other players are free to disperse and the original two players start again.

Equipment: Four cones

Progressions: Another two players have a turn and each two-person chain is timed to see how long they take to eliminate the others. The players forming the chain need to communicate with each other to move in an effective way.

drill 8

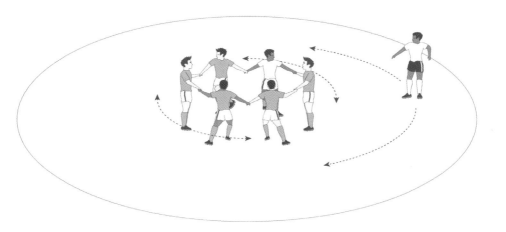

Purpose: To practise feinting with the body

Practice set-up: Four to six players link hands to form a circle with one designated player in the group. Another player is the 'chaser' and stands a few yards
away; all are in a circle 6–10 yds in diameter. The coach gives the command for the
outside player to try and tag the designated player in the circle. The other players
in the circle must hold hands without breaking free and move around in a circular
fashion to avoid the designated player being 'tagged' by the chaser. Players keep
changing roles so that they practise chasing and evading capture.

Equipment: A circle marked on the ground, one coloured bib

Progressions: Use more players holding hands so that the chaser has to move
more quickly to touch the designated player. Each player can be timed and results
compared at the end of the practice.

Purpose: Change of pace and direction when running at speed

Practice set-up: A group of players disperse in an area 15–20 yds square with two players that are identified by coloured bibs or shirts acting as the 'taggers'. The two of them chase the others, who try to evade them. Any player who is tagged must stand where he was touched with his arms outstretched to the sides and his legs wide apart like a scarecrow. The 'scarecrow' can come back into the activity if another team-mate manages to 'free' him by crawling through his legs without either of them being touched by the tagger in the process.

Equipment: Four cones, two coloured bibs

Progressions: The two players are timed on how long it takes to get everyone out in the group. Another two players then get their chance to beat the record.

Purpose: To practise reactions and quick movement

Practice set-up: An area 10–20 yds square is marked on the ground with all the players standing on one line facing the coach and bibbed out in colours making 2 teams.The coach calls or points to a line and the last person to arrive at the line designated by the coach drops a point for his team. Scores are counted up at the end of the activity.

Equipment: Four cones, two sets of coloured bibs

Progressions: The coach can develop the drill by asking the players to run to the opposite line that he points to each time. He can change his call or point to another line at any time so that the players have to react quickly. Various activities can be used to keep the players motivated (skipping, horse-and-rider, sideways run, etc.)

DRIBBLING AND RUNNING WITH THE BALL

Youngsters of between 7 and 11 tend to be somewhat oblivious of others around them as far as parting with the ball is concerned. They like to play with the ball and this should be encouraged, as the development of technical expertise is more important at this stage than learning when to dribble and when to release the ball – this will come later in the players' development. Experimentation, discovery and the repetition of a wide variety of running and dribbling movements with the ball at their feet should be a key aim for the coach. Coaches should not restrict young players at this stage by having them practice one or two 'tricks' which may be popular at that time. It is more important that they are encouraged to have a go at as wide a range of varied techniques as they can. Let them start to find their own movements as they learn to twist, stop and start with the ball.

West Ham United's attacker Carlton Cole shows elegant skill as he carries the ball past Newcastle United's Nicky Butt. The ability to run at defenders with the ball seems to be on the increase in the Premier League. (Photo: Sean Dempsey)

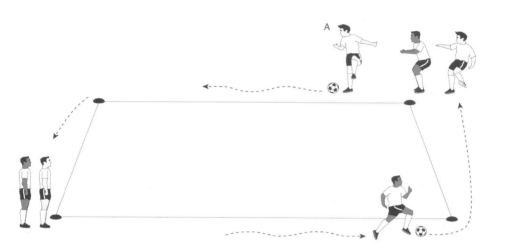

Purpose: Running straight with the ball

Practice set-up: Two files of players stand facing each other and slightly to the side, of a channel 10–20 yds long and 5 yds wide. Each file has a ball. The first player in the file proceeds to run smoothly with the ball in a straight line, and when he crosses the opposite line, the first player in the other file sets off with the ball at his feet in the opposite direction. Practise using both feet, increasing the tempo or lengthening the area so the players need to cover more distance with the ball.

Equipment: Four cones, two balls

Progressions: This drill can start with one ball only: if each player stops the ball with the sole of his foot when he reaches the line, the next player then sets off with it again. To progress the drill, players can run with the ball simultaneously from both ends until they finish a set number of repetitions – who finished first?

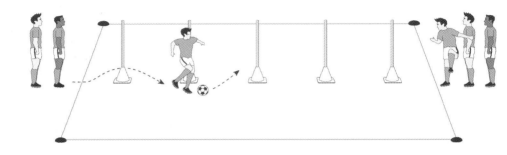

Purpose: To run with the ball while changing direction quickly

Practice set-up: The group is broken into files of players who compete against each other via a slalom course marked with flag poles placed on the ground 1–3 yds apart. Each player in turn runs with the ball through the cones in a designated fashion decided by the coach (e.g. left foot only, alternate feet, a set technique or 'trick', etc.) before their team-mate takes over from the other side. Each player has to carry out a set number of runs and the first team to finish the course wins.

Equipment: Six to eight flag poles, two cones and one ball

Progressions: The tempo can be increased or the slalom can be made 'tighter' by placing the poles closer together to increase the difficulty of the drill.

Purpose: Passing on the run with the ball

Practice set-up: A long channel 15–25 yds long by 5–10 yds wide is marked on the ground and two small goals are made with cones placed 2 yds apart. Two files of players stand at the back of their respective goals. The first player runs with the ball and tries to pass it on the run through the small goal at the other end, continuing to run and join the end of this file. The next player receives this pass and runs with the ball to the other goal and so the drill continues. Keep a few spare balls around for continuity of the practice.

Equipment: Four cones, two balls

Progressions: Both teams racing against each other at the same time. Repeat the practice in the opposite direction so players have to use both feet.

drill 14

Purpose: Dribbling and moving with the ball in all directions

Practice set-up: In the centre circle or a similar area, a group of 10–16 players dribble freely with a ball each and practise various tricks or movements. The players then try to 'tag' any other player while dribbling the ball, gaining a point for each player touched while still retaining control of their own ball. The players also avoid being tagged by dribbling with their ball quickly and skilfully to get out of danger.

Equipment: One ball per player

Progressions: A competition to see which player finishes with the least number of touches in the time-limit given; or each player touched being eliminated – the last player left wins.

Purpose: To dummy or feint at speed

Practice set-up: Two files of players, each with a ball at their feet, stand facing each other 10–20 yds apart with a cone halfway in between them. One player from each side dribbles towards the other with their ball under control. As they get within a couple of yards of the other player they dummy to go left and then take the ball past their opponent on the right side. The players then join the rear of the opposite file as the next two players approach each other. The coach needs to make sure that the players start slowly before practising the designated skill. He also needs to ensure that the players are all using the same foot and moving to the same side so that they do not collide.

Equipment: One ball per player, one cone

Progressions: Increase the tempo as players' confidence grows, and practise more difficult skills while running with the ball.

Purpose: To dribble with the ball and evade challenges

Practice set-up: A group of 12–20 players with a ball each dribble inside the centre circle or a similar area. Each player moves with his ball under control. When one player in the circle temporarily loses control of their ball, another player tries to tackle and nudge the first player's ball out of the circle. The player who loses his ball then retrieves it and rejoins the game, while the player who knocked it out gains a point. Players count their points up at the end of the session. The player with the most points wins.

Equipment: One ball per player

Progressions: All players can also gain a point by forcing another player to run his ball out of the circle by dribbling a ball towards them or each player whose ball leaves the circle is eliminated – the last player left wins.

Arsenal's Samir Nasri is shown evading the attention of West Bromwich Albion's Craig Beattie. The ability to run quickly with the ball and dribble past defenders is a great asset to teams in the modern game. (Photo: Sean Dempsey)

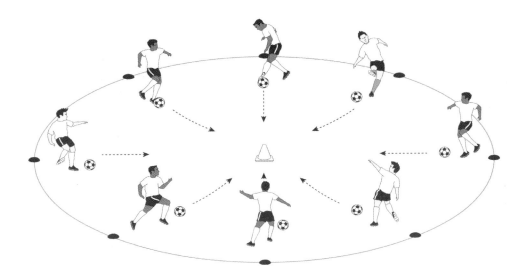

drill 17

Purpose: To practise using the inside and outside of the foot when running with the ball

Practice set-up: Eight cones are placed equal distances apart on the centre circle line. Eight players with a ball each at their feet stand at the cones, facing inwards towards the centre spot. On the coach's command, all the players run with their balls towards the centre before changing direction and doubling-back towards the next cone in a clockwise direction. The players run in sequence to the centre and then to the next cone, moving around the circuit. To increase difficulty, the coach can ensure that the players move in both directions, use both feet, speed up the tempo or practise set tricks or movements as they run with the ball.

Equipment: Nine cones, one ball per player

Progressions: As players dribble in one direction the coach can shout 'change' and the players must instantly move with the ball in the opposite direction.

Purpose: To practise beating an opponent with the ball

Practice set-up: Two files of players face a defender in a channel 10–14 yds long by 6–10 yds wide. All the attackers have a ball each and the first one dribbles the ball forwards to play 1 vs 1 with the defender, who must stay on the centre line. The attacker tries to beat the defender and arrive with the ball at the far line. When the defender is back in position, the next attacker from the other side tries to beat him as before, and so the drill continues.

Equipment: One ball per player except the defender, four cones, one coloured bib for the defender

Progressions: The coach should set a time limit of about one minute before changing the defender, as he will become easily tired. Each of the dribbling players has to fetch his own ball if the defender knocks it away, and return to the opposite line.

drill 19

Purpose: To dribble past a fast-approaching defender

Practice set-up: Two files of players face each other in a channel measuring 15 yds long by 10 yds wide. One file of players, the attackers, have a ball each. They emerge one at a time to engage a defender from the other side and try to get past him and run the ball over the far line. The defender can only move in a forward direction. After the action, both players move back to their respective files.

Equipment: Four cones, one ball between two players

Progressions: The attackers count how many points they have totalled before they become defenders. The two files compare total scores after the second file has finished attacking. At first the defenders can be 'conditioned' by not allowing them to run (walking only), tackle hard or slide-tackle. Later, as the attackers improve, the defenders are allowed to tackle for the ball as they would in a game.

drill 20

Purpose: To dribble past defenders in changing circumstances

Practice set-up: In a circle measuring 20 yds in diameter, 5–6 small goals 1–2 yds wide are marked with cones. Ten to fourteen players with a ball each play against 3–4 players who act as defenders wearing coloured bibs. The attackers try to score a point by dribbling the ball through any of the small goals (from either side of the goal) while the defenders try to prevent them from doing so.

Equipment: Ten to fourteen balls, ten to twelve cones, three to four coloured bibs

Progressions: After a timed interval of one or two minutes, the scores are tallied to find the player who has dribbled through the most goals. The defenders then swap with some of the attackers so that all players practise dribbling the ball.

PASSING THE BALL

The development of sound, natural and efficient passing techniques is an important element for youngsters at this age. If bad habits are allowed to become a part of their kicking techniques, it will be much more difficult to remove them further along the line. Young players will find some drills more difficult than others because of the technical demands involved. Players in this age range have physical limitations as well as the psychological limitations due to lack of knowledge and experience. The coach needs to be patient and find the best way of giving the younger players in this age range early passing success in the more basic skills. Brute force is not required to kick the ball effectively – the drills will enable the youngsters to practise, learn and develop a range of basic passing skills. The coach's job is to get them to concentrate on a more natural, flowing and stress-free action when passing the ball.

As before, it is essential that young players get a wide experience of passing techniques rather than repetitive practice of a few. Allow many mistakes as the youngsters practice – they will begin to learn for themselves if the coach gives them the time and encouragement to keep trying different things. It is important that the youngsters do not begin to over-rely on one foot to pass the ball. In most circumstances they will improve their game if they learn to use both feet – the coach should encourage them to do this.

Steven Gerrard, the inspirational Liverpool midfield player and captain is a devastating passer of the ball, as well as scoring many for his team – that's what makes him a great performer! (Photo: Dave Thompson)

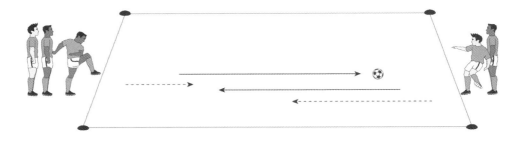

Purpose: To practise short passing using the inside and outside of the foot

Practice set-up: Two files of players face each other 8–12 yds apart. The first player in one file proceeds to pass the ball directly across to the first player in the other file and then follows it; so the drill progresses. Each player controls the ball and passes it across to the opposite side ensuring that, as they run, they go wide enough to avoid blocking the line of the next pass.

Equipment: One ball

Progressions: Use both feet and various types of passes. Later as they improve, allow them to play passes first time without controlling the ball when they feel able.

Purpose: To practise various short passes with movement

Practice set-up: Two files of players stand facing each other 10–20 yds apart. The first player on one side passes the ball to the first player on the opposite side and immediately 'peels-off' to join the back of his own file. Each player receives and passes the ball in turn before rejoining the end of their file.

Equipment: One ball

Progressions: The coach can introduce two-touch, and eventually one-touch passing.

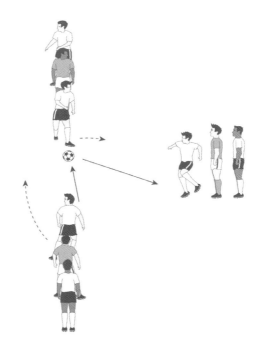

Purpose: To practise reverse passing with movement

Practice set-up: Three files are arranged in a triangular formation, each 10–15 yds apart. The first player in one file has a ball and proceeds to pass it to the next file, then follows on to join the back of that file. Each player controls and passes the ball in turn in a clockwise direction around the triangle, always following it to the next file.

Equipment: One to three balls

Progressions: The coach can introduce a second ball and third ball, both of which are passed around the triangle at the same time. He can also change the drill so the players pass in other directions and use varied passes.

Purpose: To practise short passing while moving backwards

Practice set-up: Players line up in pairs 5–10 yds apart, in a channel marked on the ground 15–25 yds long. One player in each pair has a ball and the player with the ball proceeds to pass it to the feet of his partner and they both move in the same direction, passing the ball between them. When they reach the line, they continue in the reverse direction so that both players practise passing in a forward and backward direction.

Equipment: One ball between two players, four cones

Progressions: Speed up the tempo of passing and use both feet. The players can also pass the ball whilst moving in a sideways direction.

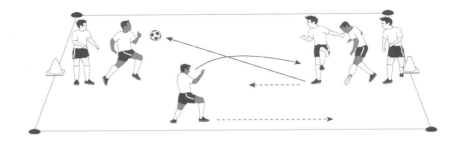

Purpose: Short volley passing

Practice set-up: Two files of players stand facing each other 6–8 yds apart, with one player holding the ball in his hands. He gently serves the ball underarm to the player opposite while quickly moving out of the way and running to the end of the opposite file. The player receiving the ball passes it on the volley, cushioning it so the pass arrives for the next player to catch. He then moves to the back of the opposite file and so the drill continues, with one side tossing the ball while the other side passes on the volley.

Equipment: One ball, two cones

Progressions: Players practise using their weaker foot and serving the ball with spin, which is a more difficult skill.

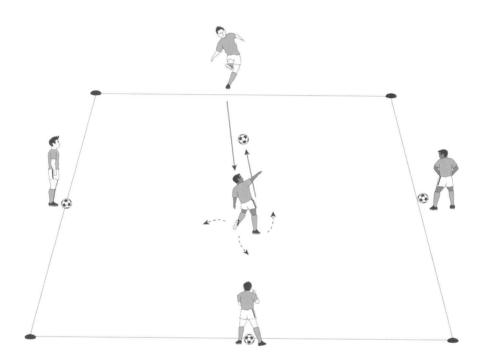

Purpose: To practise short passing with the inside and outside of both feet

Practice set-up: Four players with a ball each at their feet stand in a cross formation facing a fifth player, who stands without a ball in the middle. The players are 5–10 yds apart and the first player passes the ball to the central player for him to control and pass straight back. The central player then turns to the next player in rotation to receive a pass, and so the drill progresses for a set time interval or number of passes before changing places with another player.

Equipment: Four cones, four balls

Progressions: Change direction, feet and tempo of the drill by asking players to play first-time passes when they are able to do so.

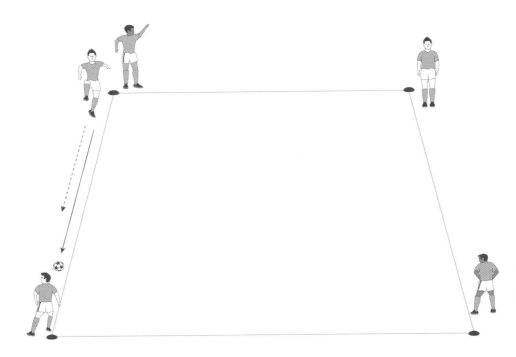

Purpose: Short passing and movement

Practice set-up: Five players stand at the corners of a 10–15 yd square. Two of them stand together at one corner while the other three players position themselves at the other corners. One of the two players standing together has a ball and passes it to the player on the next corner while following on in the same direction to change places with him as that player controls and passes it on in turn. Each player controls and passes the ball while moving in stages around the square.

Equipment: Four cones, one ball

Progressions: Move in both directions, and groups can compete to see who can pass around the square quickest after a set number of circuits.

Purpose: Using alternate feet rhythmically to pass the ball

Practice set-up: Three players form a triangle 3–6 yds apart. One player without a ball faces two others who each have a ball at their feet. Both players pass alternately and continuously to the middle player who returns the passes first time in a rhythmical way, using his right and left feet.

Equipment: Two balls

Progressions: Each player in turn has a set time or number of passes and the tempo of the passes should be gradually increased.

drill 29

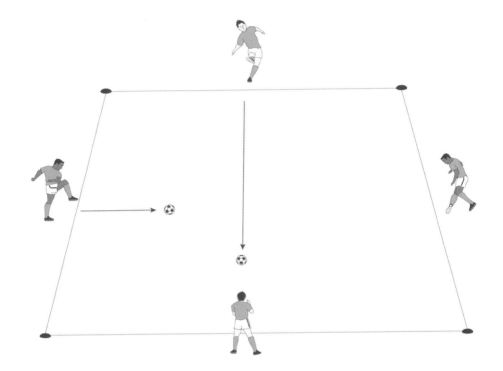

Purpose: To practise control and timing of short passes

Practice set-up: Four players form a cross in a 8–12 yd square. Two players have a ball and pass it directly to their partner opposite, who controls it before quickly passing it back. All the players need to keep their passing sequence going and avoid striking the other ball as they do so.

Equipment: Two balls, four cones

Progressions: Use both feet, varied techniques and increase the tempo to first-time passes when they are ready. Count the highest sequence of passes attained before it breaks down – this is the record, try and beat it!

drill 30

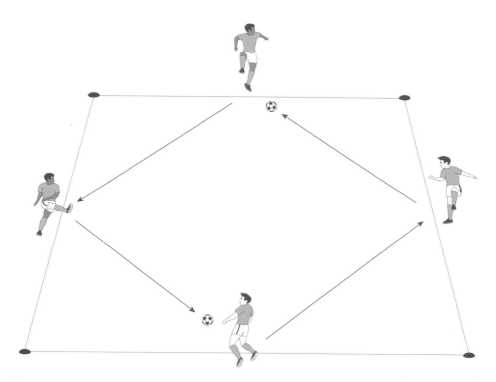

Purpose: Quick passing and control

Practice set-up: Four players stand around a 10–15 yd square, two of them with a ball at their feet. The two players with a ball proceed to pass the ball simultaneously in a clockwise direction around the square, so the balls rotate. At first, players should control the ball before passing it, but later they should try to pass the ball straightaway so that the balls are continually on the move.

Equipment: Four cones, two balls

Progressions: Use both feet in both directions. The coach can suddenly call 'change' whereupon all the players need to quickly change the direction of their passing.

Purpose: Short passing and controlling the ball

Practice set-up: Two players stand approximately 7–10 yards apart, one with a ball at his foot. A small goal about 2–3 feet wide is set up in the centre with poles. The player with the ball passes the ball directly through the goal to the other player who receives it, controls the ball to the side of the pole and passes it down the side of the goal back to the first player who is in a central position. He then controls the ball and the process starts again.

Equipment: One ball and two posts

Progressions: Ask the player controlling the ball to move to alternate sides each time using both right and left feet. Players are only allowed 2 or 3 touches of the ball before passing. Keep changing the players over so they have spells as passers and controllers.

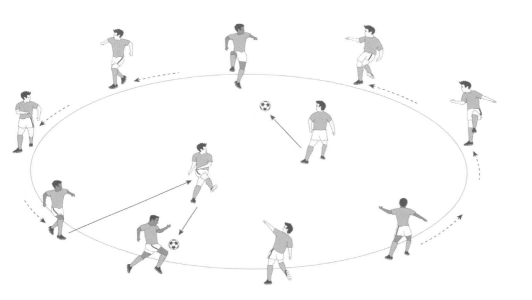

Purpose: Short passing on the move

Practice set-up: Six to ten players stand around the centre circle, or similar area, with two players who have a ball each at their feet facing them from the centre. The outside players jog around the circle in the same direction while the two central players, who stand a little apart from each other, pass the ball to each player in turn. The players give them a quick return pass, so that they pass around the circle in sequence.

Equipment: Two balls

Progressions: Pass in each direction, increase the tempo and change players' roles so that they all get turns in the centre and on the outside of the circle.

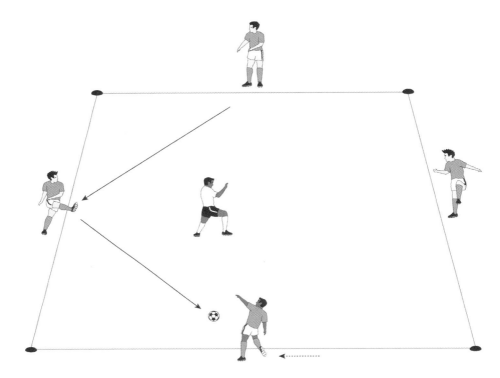

Purpose: Controlling and timing passes

Practice set-up: A cone is placed on each corner of a 10 yd square. One player stands in the middle, and four others stand on the outside of the four sides with one ball between them. The four players proceed to interpass, ensuring that they do not go inside the square, but that the ball passes through the square and inside their own cones each time. The middle player cannot leave his area, but tries to intercept each pass.

Equipment: Four cones, one coloured bib, one ball

Progressions: To increase the difficulty of the drill, the players can be restricted to two or three touches only. Alternatively, if their pass is cut out or goes astray, they change places with the defender.

drill 34

Purpose: Timing and selection of passes

Practice set-up: In a square 12 x 12 yds in area, four or five players play against one defender and try to maintain possession of the ball. The four players can move around anywhere in the area while the defender tries to intercept the ball.

Equipment: Four cones, one coloured bib, one ball

Progressions: The coach can impose conditions such as two touches only, or reduce the number of attackers, or even add another defender to increase the difficulty of the drill.

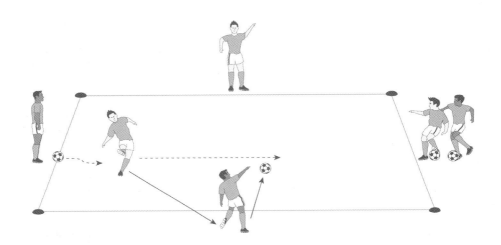

Purpose: Wall-passing

Practice set-up: Two files of players with a ball each stand 15–20 yds apart, and two players stand at the halfway mark 10 yds apart. The first player from one side plays a pass directly to one of the two central players, who relays it straight back to the passer while he is running to the other side. This player then controls the ball and runs with it to the back of the opposite file. The next player then repeats the process to the other central player, thus playing a 'wall-pass' in the opposite direction.

Equipment: Four cones, one ball per player, except the two central players

Progressions: The players can pass simultaneously so two players are 'wall-passing' from both sides at the same time.

SHOOTING AT GOAL

For youngsters this is a very exciting element of the game and one for which they need to learn the correct mechanics of kicking the ball. Young players naturally want to score goals, as indeed players of any age do. However, it is at this early age that the boy's peers, coaches or parents can unconsciously begin to put pressure on him to score and this will affect the development of his technique. This is often reflected by players 'tightening-up', which affects muscular co-ordination and can result in them trying to smash the ball out of the stadium, when in fact a calmer approach would have helped and allowed them to hit the target! The coach needs to help players to concentrate on smoothness and style when shooting at goal – the process is more important than the end result at this stage. Young players see this as an enjoyable part of the game and love to practice it – however the coach should play down excessive goal celebrations when someone scores. It is a bad habit that has appeared in the game which needs to be controlled. Scoring a goal should be sufficient satisfaction in itself!

Liverpool's Fernando Torres, seen here going past Stoke City's Seyi Olofinjana, is a deadly goalscorer and a good striker of the ball. (Photo: Dave Thompson)

Purpose: Shooting from a wall-pass

Practice set-up: A file of players with a ball each stands at the edge of the penalty area facing the coach who is 10 yds away. A goalkeeper defends the goal with two ball-retrievers stationed behind and to each side. Each player, in turn, passes the ball directly to the coach, who returns it directly to the right or left side so the player who has run on to the ball can shoot at goal. The player collects the ball from the retrievers and rejoins the end of the file as the drill continues.

Equipment: One ball per player

Progressions: Change the shooting angles and shoot from a greater distance. Remember the importance of using both feet.

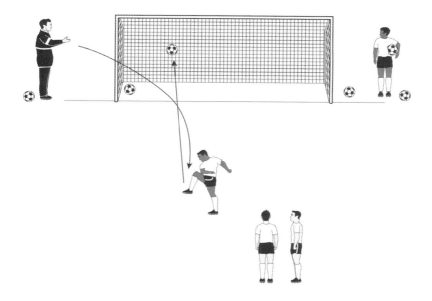

Purpose: To practise short volley and half-volley shooting

Practice set-up: Two servers with a supply of footballs stand to the side of a goal with fixed nets. They are faced by a small file of players 4–8 yds away. The servers toss the ball underarm to each player in turn and the player hits a volley or half-volley into the net before returning to the back of the file. Servers should toss the ball at the correct pace to maintain the practice flow.

Equipment: A good supply of balls, a goal with a practice net or a rebound surface

Progressions: Count the number of goals the players score in the empty goal in a timed interval or in a set number of services.

drill 38

Purpose: Quick reactions when shooting

Practice set-up: Two files of players face a goal 10–20 yds away, being defended by a goalkeeper. The coach is in a central position with a supply of balls. The first two players sit down and the coach serves the ball in between them so that they can recover quickly from their position. The first one to the ball gets to shoot at goal. They retrieve their ball as the next two repeat the process.

Equipment: A good supply of balls

Progressions: The coach can make the service more difficult or speed up the process by serving the ball more quickly.

drill 39

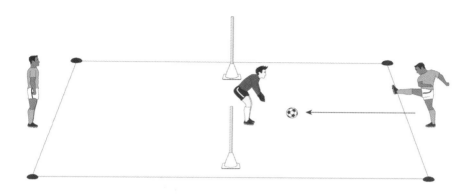

Purpose: Shooting with the instep of the foot

Practice set-up: In a channel measuring 30 yds long by 10 yds wide a makeshift goal using flag poles is erected with a goalkeeper guarding the 'sticks'. One player stands at each end of the channel, one with a ball at his feet. The goalkeeper faces the player in possession of the ball, who shoots at goal. If the keeper saves the shot, he feeds it to the other player; if the shot goes past him, he turns to face the next shot.

Equipment: Two flag poles, four cones, one ball

Progressions: The players have a competition to see who scores most goals within a time-limit.

Purpose: To get in a shot against a recovering defender

Practice set-up: Two files of players stand in pairs 12–15 yds away from and to each side of the goal. One player has a ball and the other player, the 'defender', stands with his back to the goal with his legs apart. The player with the ball faces the defender and proceeds to push the ball through his legs, then runs around him quickly to shoot at the goal as the defender recovers.

Equipment: One ball between two players

Progressions: The players shoot from alternate sides and change over roles and sides after a timed interval so that everyone gets a taste of the action.

drill 41

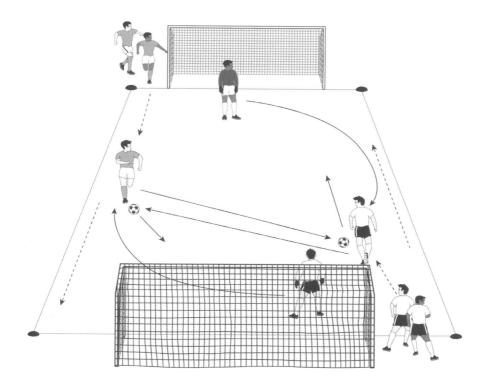

Purpose: To strike a moving ball at goal

Practice set-up: Two goals, defended by goalkeepers, are erected on an area measuring 25 yds long by 15 yds wide. The goalkeepers have a good ball supply in their goals. Two files of players stand next to each goal, but on opposite sides. The goalkeepers throw the ball simultaneously to the first player in the file on the opposite side. Each player controls the ball before passing it to the first player from the opposite file so they can shoot at goal. The two players then retire to the end of the file at the other side and the goalkeepers throw the ball to the next two players, and so the drill continues.

Equipment: Two portable goals, four cones, a good supply of balls

Progressions: Players can only shoot with the weakest foot or try to hit a certain area of the goal (e.g. low at far post).

Purpose: To shoot alternately with both feet

Practice set-up: Six to eight balls are placed in a line 1 yard apart and 10–15 yds from a goal defended by a goalkeeper. A line of players face the balls and the first player starts by running and striking the outside ball on the right with his right foot before quickly moving to strike the ball on his extreme left side with his left foot. He moves like a pendulum from the outside in until he has hit all the balls at goal.

Equipment: Six to eight balls

Progressions: Count the player's scoring ratio and how fast he achieves this, and compare it with other players.

drill 43

Purpose: Shooting from a narrow angle

Practice set-up: Six to eight balls are laid on the ground a yard apart and at an angle 10–15 yds from the goal. A file of players stands behind and to the side of the ball furthest from the goal. Each player runs to the line of balls and hits each ball in turn, moving down or up the line according to the coach's instructions, and looking to shoot all balls rhythmically and quickly. The coach can impose a time-limit, each player needing to take all shots within that interval. The player can use various techniques to score, such as out-swinging shots or swerved shots.

Equipment: Six to eight balls

Progressions: The drill is flexible, and the coach can ask the player to hit with one foot only or both feet. The coach can number the balls so that the player needs to react at speed when the coach calls the numbers, in order to shoot at goal as quickly as possible.

drill 44

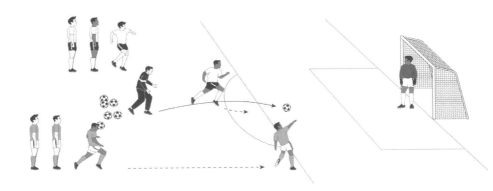

Purpose: To get in a shot while under challenge

Practice set-up: Two files of players line up 5 yds apart and 10–15 yds from a goal defended by a goalkeeper. The coach stands in a central position with a supply of balls and proceeds to pass the ball each time to one file, whose players look to get their shots in while the players from the other side give chase and try to prevent the shot. After a set period the players change roles. The coach should ensure that all players receive practice in shooting with both feet.

Equipment: A good supply of balls

Progressions: The service can be made more difficult for the player shooting by playing the ball nearer to the defender.

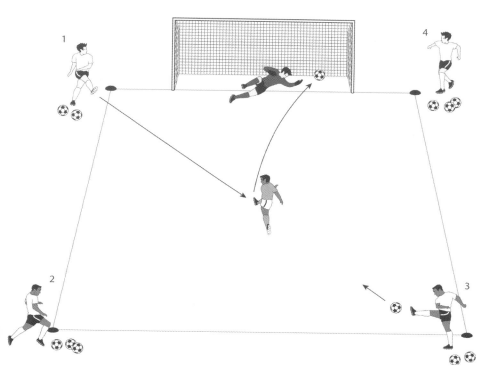

Purpose: Shooting in a variety of circumstances

Practice set-up: Four players each with three balls at their feet stand on the corners of a 10–20 yd square, with a player in the centre facing a goal defended by a goalkeeper. The players pass the ball in rotation for the central player to control and shoot quickly at goal. The players then switch positions after all twelve balls have been served so that a new player is given practice in the central position.

Equipment: Four cones, twelve balls

Progressions: The coach can make it more competitive by adding scores, only allowing first-time shots or asking the servers to toss the ball in the air for the central player to hit volleys or half-volleys.

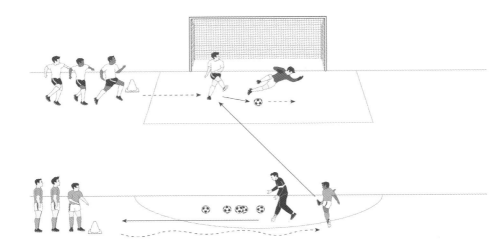

Purpose: To decide where to shoot at goal

Practice set-up: Two files of players stand opposite each other 10 yds to one side of the goal and 14–16 yds apart. The file nearest to the goal are the defenders; the file furthest from the goal are the attackers. The coach stands in front of the goal and in line with the file of attackers with a supply of footballs. He faces the file of attackers and passes to each one in turn. The attacker controls the ball and quickly runs with it to go around the coach and shoot as fast as he can. As soon as the coach passes the ball a defender moves to cover his goal line as the goalkeeper 'narrows the shooting angle' in front of him. Both players move back to their respective files and the drill continues.

Equipment: Two cones, a good supply of balls

Progressions: Change roles of attackers and defenders after a set period of time and encourage the attackers to assess the situation before deciding where to shoot. For example, the player may chip the ball over the goalkeeper's head, away from the covering defender.

drill 47

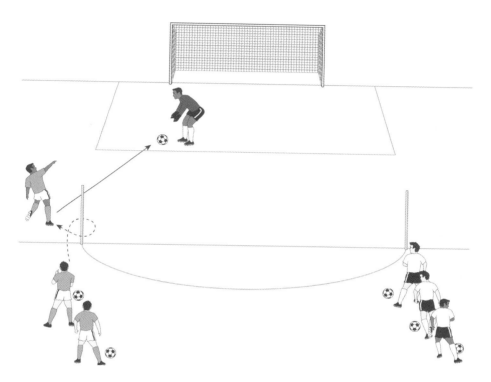

Purpose: To shoot on the turn

Practice set-up: Two files of players stand to the side of each other 16–20 yds from a goal, with two flag poles placed in the ground a few yards in front. The players, who each have a ball at their feet, run forwards alternately at speed, going completely around the pole with the ball before shooting on the turn at goal. The players retrieve their balls as the next players come forwards to dribble the ball round the poles before shooting. Make sure players shoot as soon as they are coming out of the turn and change poles alternately so that they shoot from both sides using both feet.

Equipment: Two flag poles, a good supply of balls

Progressions: Two teams can compete against each other within a time-limit to see who scores the most goals.

drill 48

Purpose: To dribble and shoot

Practice set-up: Two players, an attacker and defender, stand in a channel in the penalty area 10–12 yds wide with six balls placed in the penalty arc. The attacker collects a ball and dribbles it past the defender to try and score. If he does they swap roles. The defender gets a ball and attacks while the attacker defends and they compete to see who can score most goals. If the defender wins the ball in the area he can go on to score; either way the players have alternate opportunities each time to defend or attack.

Equipment: Four cones, six balls

Progressions: The player with the ball must dribble past the defender before scoring.

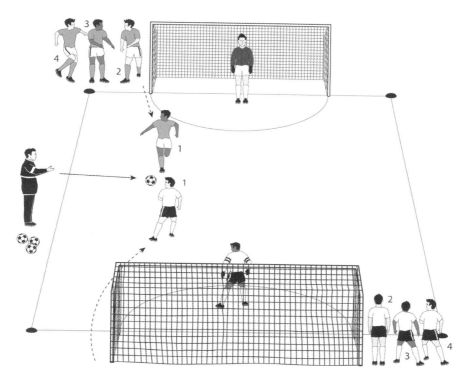

Purpose: Dribbling and shooting at goal

Practice set-up: On an area 25 yds long by 20 yds wide, two goals are erected and manned by goalkeepers. A small 'keepers only' semi-circle area is marked in front of each goal. Two files of players are bibbed out in two different colours to identify them and are numbered. The two teams sit behind a goal each and the coach calls a number and feeds a ball into the area. The two players play 1 vs 1 and try to beat their opponent and score. As soon as the coach calls a new number, the two players must leave the ball and return to sit behind their goals while the next two players compete.

Equipment: One ball, two sets of coloured bibs, two portable goals

Progressions: The team with the most goals wins. Later the coach can call two numbers so that the game becomes 2 v 2.

drill 50

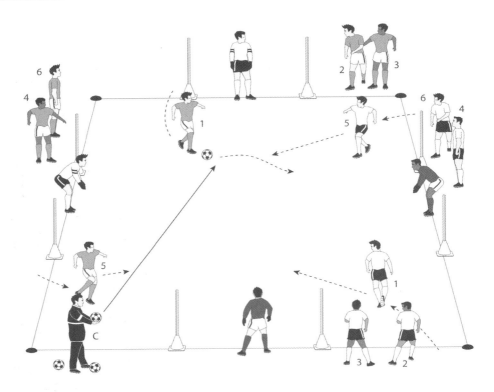

Purpose: To dribble past a player before shooting

Practice set-up: A 15 yd square area is marked out with four goals positioned centrally on each side, which are defended by goalkeepers. Two adjacent goals are defended by goalkeepers from one team and two by goalkeepers from the other team. Two groups of six players in coloured bibs are split into two smaller teams that are numbered 1, 2, 3 and 4, 5, 6 respectively. Each team of three players sits behind their respective goals and opposite the opposing team with the same numbers. The coach calls two numbers, always an odd and even, and feeds a ball into the area. The four numbered players play 2 vs 2. Each pair has to defend their two goals and can score in either of the opposing goals. Whatever two numbers the coach calls, four players come out to try and score each time.

Equipment: Four cones, two portable goals, two balls, two sets of coloured bibs numbered from one to six (or as required)

Progressions: Count the goals scored within a time limit.

HEADING THE BALL

This is one of the most neglected skills in the game and one that requires careful handling when presented to youngsters for the first time. Heading is hardly a natural technique – your first reaction is to shut your eyes and move your head out of the way of the ball as it approaches! It is vital in the early stages of their development for young players to feel confident that heading the ball will not be a painful experience.

For this reason, light-weight balls should be used, with the accent on fun and variety to alleviate any fears that youngsters have of heading the ball. The drills provided will enable the players to build up their technical expertise gradually before moving on to the more difficult skill of heading from crosses from the flanks. Because many young players are unable to chip, cross or drive the ball through the air with consistent accuracy, they do not get practice or experience in heading the ball. This means that the practice situation needs to be supplemented in some way.

Liverpool's Xabi Alonso towers above Manchester United's Paul Scholes to get in an effective header, even though he is under pressure. (Photo: Mike Egerton)

drill 51

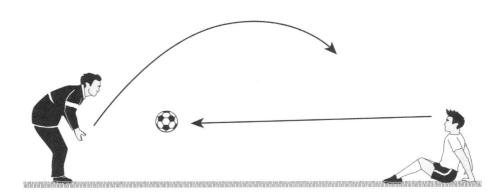

Purpose: Body power for heading

Practice set-up: A player sits on the ground facing his partner, who stands 3–6 yds away with a ball in his hands. The server tosses the ball gently underarm for the sitting player to return with a chest-high header, which the server catches. Players change positions after a set number of headers.

Equipment: One ball

Progressions: As the player improves, the server can throw the ball from a longer distance, so that more power and accuracy is required. The server can also move around to provide a moving target for the player heading the ball. Make sure the ball is served a little short of the sitting player so that he can gain power from his neck and body to head it back to the server.

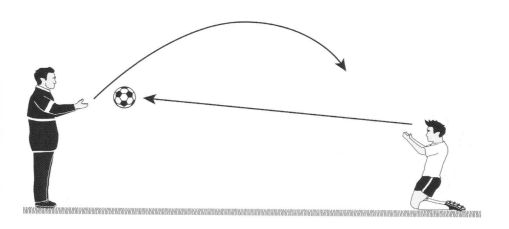

Purpose: Using the body to head the ball more effectively

Practice set-up: Two players face each other 3–5 yds apart, one standing with a ball in his hands while the other kneels on the ground. The server tosses the ball underarm, using both hands, for the kneeling player to return with a chest-high header. By denying the player the use of his legs when kneeling, he has to use his upper body more effectively to generate power to the ball. Players change positions after a set number of headers. Ensure the ball is served 'short' of the player.

Equipment: One ball

Progressions: Move further away when serving so that the player has to utilise more power when heading the ball.

Purpose: Diving header

Practice set-up: Two players face each other, one standing holding the ball and the other kneeling on the ground 3–5 yds away on soft ground in an extended position or on a cushioned mat. The server tosses the ball underarm dropping it short of the kneeling player so that he needs to dive to head the ball. Ensure the player heading the ball uses both hands in front of himself to cushion his contact with the ground. The header should be played so that the server can catch it each time. Players change positions after a set number of headers.

Equipment: One ball

Progressions: The server can drop the ball even shorter or stand further away as he serves. Either way it will increase the difficulty for the other player who is diving to head the ball.

drill 54

Purpose: Controlled heading

Practice set-up: A file of players face a team-mate who stands 3–5 yds away with a ball in his hands. The server tosses the ball underarm to the first player in the file, who returns it with an accurate header for the server to catch. The first player then crouches down while the server tosses the ball over his head for the next player in the file to head back and crouch down in turn. When he has moved along the file, the server joins the front of the file and the back player becomes the server. Proceed until everyone has had a turn.

Equipment: One ball

Progressions: Set up teams to compete against each other. Only headers that are caught by the server count. The ball must be served in sequence until all the players have successfully returned it.

drill 55

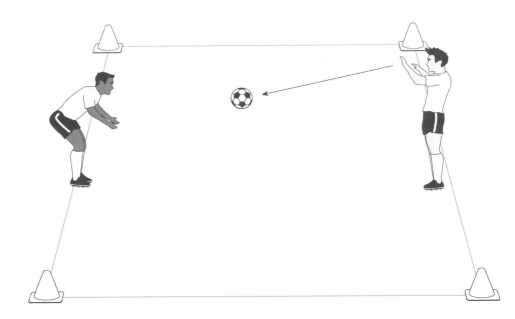

Purpose: Heading for accuracy and power

Practice set-up: Using cones, set up two makeshift goals 5–10 yds wide and 5–10 yds apart. A player stands in the middle of each goal. One of the players tosses the ball up for himself and tries to score in the other goal with a header while the other player acts as a goalkeeper and tries to save the ball. He then serves himself and tries to score with a header. Players can score with a direct header from wherever they catch the ball. The drill should flow with headers and saves – count the goals to find the winner.

Equipment: Four cones, one ball

Progressions: Move the goals further away from each other so that the headers require more power. Allow players to head directly from an opponent's header either by diving or jumping to surprise the player.

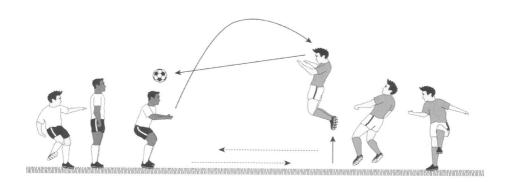

Purpose: Jumping to head the ball

Practice set-up: Two files of players stand facing each other 5–10 yds apart and slightly to the side of each other. The first player tosses the ball underarm to the first player on the other side, then quickly turns and joins the back of his own file. The player receiving the ball jumps and heads it directly into the hands of the second player on the opposite file, then turns to run to the back of his own file. The sequence continues so that one file serves while the other heads the ball. Make sure that the balls are served high. Once the first player is back at the start, the files change over.

Equipment: One ball

Progressions: The files move further apart so that the players heading the ball have greater difficulty in judging the ball's flight and in maintaining accuracy. Count the highest sequence of successful headers and try to beat this record each time.

drill 57

Purpose: Controlled heading

Practice set-up: The player gently tosses the ball to himself and heads it so that it rebounds from a wall for him to catch. He continues to feed the ball to himself, attempting to head it twice in succession before catching it and so on, increasing the number of headers by one each time. (Beware of standing too near the wall.) Ensure the player heads through the lower half of the ball.

Equipment: One ball, a high wall or a vertical rebound surface

Progressions: Each time the player practises he tries to beat his record score.

Purpose: Controlled and 'touch' heading

Practice set-up: A player faces a wall and gently tosses the ball high against it so that the ball rebounds. The player attempts to keep the ball in the air by repeatedly heading it against the wall. To improve control, the player should move closer to the wall until he can place both hands against it while still heading the ball rhythmically against the wall. (Beware of standing too near the wall.)

Equipment: One ball, a high wall or vertical rebound surface

Progressions: Start to move further from and then nearer to the wall while heading the ball, keeping control of it in the process. In this way the player will learn to have good 'touch' of the ball. Always be aware of the safety element and ensure the players don't attempt to head the ball if too near the wall.

Purpose: Heading for defending

Practice set-up: The player marks a line on a wall above his head. He faces the wall and either tosses the ball up to head it or tosses it underarm directly against the wall to head it. The player should start a heading sequence, counting only the headers which go above the line and try to beat his record.

Equipment: One ball and a high wall

Progressions: Players need to learn to head the ball high and away from the goal. Make the line on the wall higher – but not so high that players find it difficult to reach it with a header.

drill 60

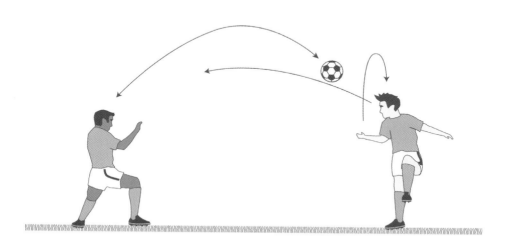

Purpose: 'Touch' heading

Practice set-up: Two players stand 2–5 yds apart, one with a ball in his hands. He carefully tosses the ball upwards towards himself and heads it high and accurately for the other player to return with a header which the first player catches. This counts as two consecutive headers. The first player then repeats as before, however, the players now attempt three consecutive headers and the second player catches the ball. The players try to move up to 10 or more headers.

Equipment: One ball

Progressions: The two players move further apart so that greater accuracy is required when heading the ball.

drill 61

Purpose: 'Touch' heading

Practice set-up: One player stands on his own, holding the ball. He gently and accurately tosses the ball upwards for himself and, keeping his head back, heads the ball skywards before catching it. He then tries to head it twice successively, then three times and so on.

Equipment: One ball

Progressions: Players continually try to beat their personal best score.

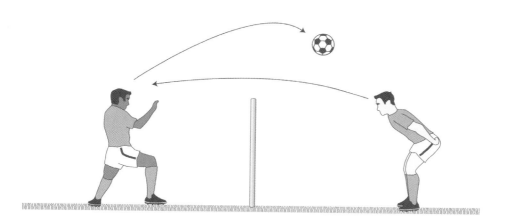

Purpose: Controlled heading

Practice set-up: Put up a 3–5 ft high long net or rope. A line of players pairs up on each side of it, with one ball between each pair. Each player with a ball starts by gently heading the ball over the net or rope for his partner to head back, so they can keep up a sequence. Later partners can pair up against other pairs (2 vs 2) on the same net. Place a mark on the ground to divide the area in half.

Equipment: One ball, two flag poles, a rope or net

Progressions: Each pair competes against another pair to see who can attain the highest heading sequence.

Purpose: Controlled heading on the move

Practice set-up: Put up a net or rope 3–5 ft high and 1–2 yds wide. Two files of players stand on either side of it, facing each other, one file with a ball. The first player starts by tossing the ball across the net for the player opposite to head straight back over again for the next player opposite to catch. Both players – the thrower and the player heading the ball – run around the net to join the back of the opposite file as the drill continues.

Equipment: One ball, two flag poles, a rope or net

Progressions: Teams compete against each other and count their highest consecutive score.

Purpose: Leaping to head the ball from a standing jump

Practice set-up: The coach, or a player, holds the ball in both hands high above the head of a player who is standing. The player underneath the ball springs up repeatedly, using both legs, to head the ball that is held by the coach. As they head the ball the players should tighten their neck muscles. After six jumps the player moves to the end of the file and the next player starts. The player holding the ball in the air can use a box to stand on if more height is needed.

Equipment: One ball, one box (if necessary) for the coach/player to stand on

Progressions: The coach holds the ball a little higher each time so that the player needs more spring to reach the ball.

Purpose: Jumping to head the ball on the run

Practice set-up: Players stand in a file facing the coach, who holds the ball in both hands in the air. They run in sequence and jump using one leg to take off and head the ball, which is cushioned in the coach's grip. The player returns to the back of the file as the next player takes his turn.

Equipment: One ball

Progressions: The coach should hold the ball higher as the players' jumping ability increases.

Purpose: To withstand body contact when jumping

Practice set-up: Two files of players stand side-on and a short distance apart. With the coach in front they keep in order and jog slowly forwards towards a cone 20 yds away. On the coach's command of 'Up!', they jump and make contact with the sides of their shoulders. When they reach the cone they jog backwards and then repeat the exercise.

Equipment: Two cones

Progressions: The coach must ensure the practice is safe and the contact between players is sensible.

drill 67

Purpose: Jumping to head the ball

Practice set-up: The coach faces a file of players standing 6–8 yds away. The coach feeds the first player with a high, soft and looping service and the player comes forwards, jumps and heads the ball back accurately before returning to the back of the file. The coach then serves continuously to each player in turn. He should keep some spare balls at his feet for misdirected headers.

Equipment: One ball (a few spare balls should be available)

Progressions: Throw the ball a little higher each time, so that the players need to improve their timing and increase their power when heading the ball.

Purpose: Defensive power heading

Practice set-up: A file of players faces the coach from a distance of 3–5 yds, with two ball-retrievers facing the back of the coach behind a cone the same distance away. The coach tosses the ball to the first player who heads it high and long over the coach's head for one of the retrievers to catch. The player then turns and runs to the back of the file while the next player receives a service from the coach. Change the ball-retrievers often.

Equipment: Two cones, one ball (a few spare balls should be available)

Progressions: Increase the distances of the players and ball-retrievers from the coach to improve the power and distance when heading. (Remember to use a lighter weight football.)

Purpose: Power heading in defence

Practice set-up: A coach stands facing a player who is 3–5 yds away. Behind the coach are a series of lines or cones set at yard intervals to represent distances. The first one is placed 1–2 yds behind the coach. A ball-retriever stands within the lines or cones to measure the distance of the headed ball. The coach serves the ball underarm and the player heads it as far over the coach's head as he can, getting points for the distance achieved. The ball-retriever returns the ball to the coach. The player gets six headers, totalling his score before changing places with the ball-retriever.

Equipment: Six cones, one ball

Progressions: Each player continually looks to improve his score. As players improve the coach can serve the ball higher, so that the player needs to spring higher when heading the ball.

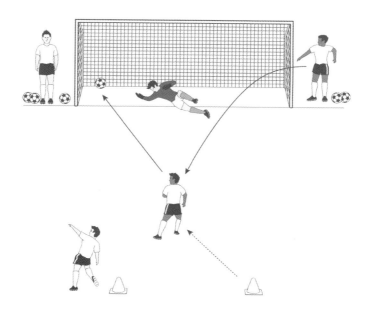

Purpose: Glancing headers

Practice set-up: Two servers stand at the sides of the goal with six balls each. The goalkeeper stands on the goal line while two players stand 6–8 yds in front and behind two cones in line with the goalposts. The servers alternately toss the balls gently underarm in a diagonal direction for each player to come and head at goal. After heading the ball the player runs towards the other cone as the next player receives service. The goalkeeper must stay on the goal line when defending the goal.

Equipment: Two cones, a good supply of balls

Progressions: Encourage the servers to make the practice more difficult by tossing the ball so the players need to jump high, or dive, to head the ball at goal. Make it more competitive – who scores most goals?

Aston Villa's emerging young striker, Gabriel Agbonlahov, scores against Manchester City. He is fast becoming a 'provider' for others in his team as well as becoming an accomplished scorer in his own right. (Photo: Nick Potts)

CROSSING AND FINISHING

Although an integral part of the game, the techniques of crossing the ball and finishing off the resultant cross with a shot or header are difficult for young players to learn. With this in mind, the coach needs to be patient and aware of the potential difficulties so that he can guide the youngsters more sensitively through the drills.

Young players who can kick the ball reasonably well when striking it in a straightforward direction find it much more difficult to kick a ball on the move when they have to lift it up to a team-mate's head while running in another direction. The necessary balance, timing and co-ordination of several limbs needs much practice before the technique becomes refined. Equally difficult is the skill of moving on to a fast-approaching ball and timing it so that the player hits it on the ground, or in the air with a volley, or heads it at goal.

By using the drills and modifying them where necessary, such as allowing the players to cross a stationary ball, or by using a bigger or lighter ball, or controlling the cross before shooting, the players' confidence will grow and the coach can gradually increase the tempo as they progress. As has been mentioned earlier, it is important that youngsters get good quality practice of these skills which are linked – you can't do one without the other. Most players are more confident either crossing the ball with a certain preferred foot or from a certain side of the field. We are all stronger at heading the ball from one flank rather than another. With this in mind, it is important for the coach to set up practices from both sides of the field.

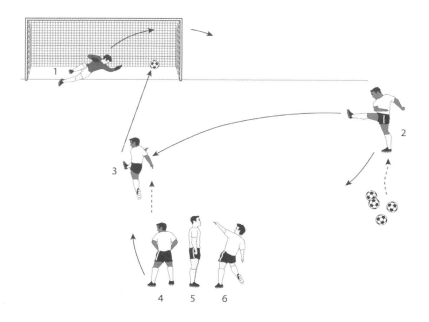

Purpose: Shooting from a cross

Practice set-up: A group of players are numbered from 1 to 5 or 6 with 1 acting as goalkeeper, 2 acting as the crosser and 3 shooting at goal from 10–15 yds, while the others form a file behind. Number 2 has a good supply of balls and proceeds either to play a ball along the ground or cross it in the air for number 3 to control and shoot at goal. All three players rotate so that 3 becomes the goalkeeper, 1 is the crosser and 2 joins the end of the file while 4 comes forwards to shoot.

Equipment: A good supply of balls

Progressions: Cross from both sides before shooting, or have the crosser position himself closer to the touchline, to increase the difficulty for the player shooting.

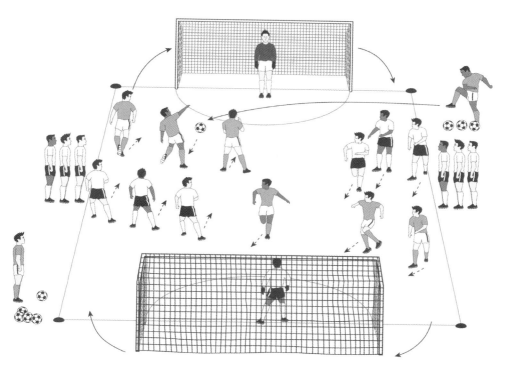

Purpose: Crossing and heading practice

Practice set-up: On an area 20 yds long by 30 yds wide, two goals are defended by goalkeepers. Two groups of three players stand at the halfway mark and two groups of three players stand in opposite corners. A server stands in the other two corners with a good supply of balls. The servers cross the ball to the corner groups in turn as they try to score. The four groups jog around the back of the goals and rotate around the area to continually meet the cross from the server for a set time-limit. All the groups add up their goal count.

Equipment: Four cones, two portable goals, a good supply of balls

Progressions: Keep changing around so that all players have equal opportunities to cross and head the ball.

drill 73

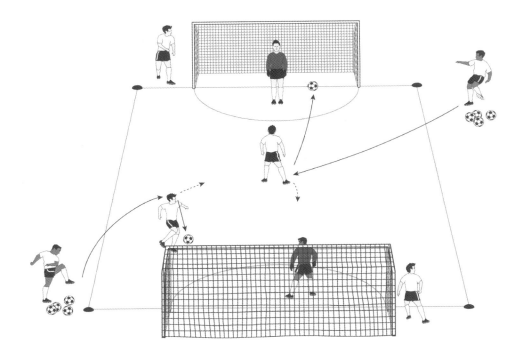

Purpose: Crossing to a specific area

Practice set-up: On an area measuring 20–25 yds long by 30 yds wide, two portable goals are positioned with a goalkeeper in each one. Two players acting as wingers stand in opposite corners with a good supply of balls. Two players acting as strikers face one goal each. A ball-retriever stands behind each goal. One winger crosses a low ball while the other crosses a high service each time so that each striker shoots or heads at goal before they turn and bypass each other to attack the other goal. They receive heading and shooting practice in this drill for a set interval before changing with other players.

Equipment: Four cones, two portable goals, a good supply of balls

Progressions: Players continually change their roles, acting as wingers, strikers, or ball-retrievers.

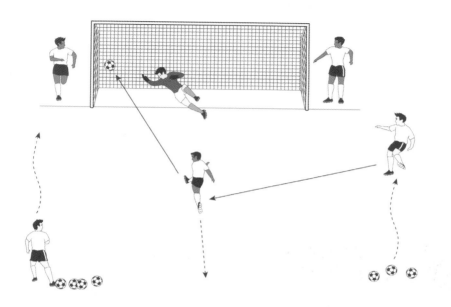

Purpose: Cutting the ball back on the move for a player to shoot

Practice set-up: A striker faces a goal 15–20 yds away which is defended by a goalkeeper. Two wingers stand 15–20 yds away from the goal with a good supply of balls. Two ball-retrievers are positioned behind the goal. The wingers run with the ball before cutting it back for the striker to finish with headers or shots. Depending on the type of service, the player can control the ball before shooting, volley the ball in the air, or head the ball at goal. The striker should change with another player after a set interval. The service should be regular.

Equipment: A good supply of balls

Progressions: The player cutting the ball back should be encouraged to run more quickly with the ball and to cross on the move, while the striker is allowed one touch to strike at goal. After a set period the ball retrievers become wingers, the wingers become strikers, and the strikers become ball retrievers.

drill 75

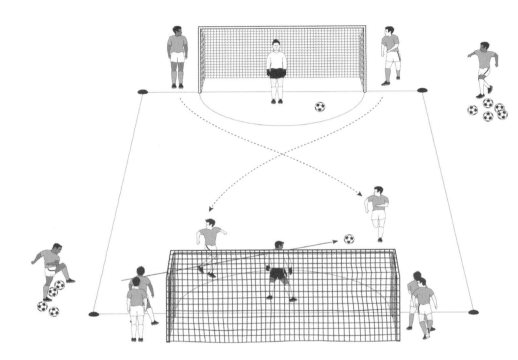

Purpose: Learning to time runs at goal and finish effectively

Practice set-up: Two portable goals, with goalkeepers, are positioned 20–30 yds apart, and two servers stand in opposite corners with a good supply of balls. Four pairs of players line up in files at the sides of each goal. Pairs of players come forwards alternately from each side to receive a thrown service from each server which they try to convert to goals. The pair perform a crossover run before receiving the service, and the server can vary the service by rolling it along the ground or tossing it higher for a header. The pair of players retires to the far file as the drill continues in the opposite direction. The goalkeepers must stay in their goal areas and not move forwards to stop the crosses.

Equipment: Four cones, a good supply of balls

Progressions: Ensure players continually change to get crossing and heading practice and eventually ask the servers to serve the ball by volleying it from their hands.

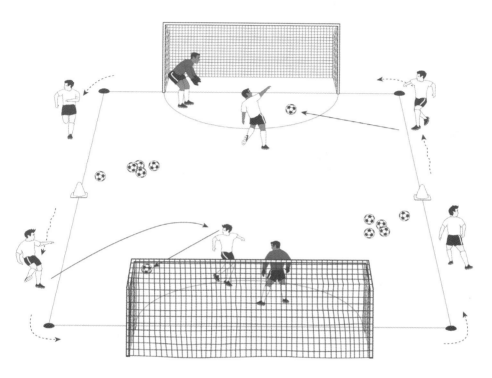

Purpose: Crossing and finishing in rotation

Practice set-up: Two portable goals are erected on an area measuring 25 yds square, both guarded by a goalkeeper. A supply of balls is left on the centre line on both sides. Two players run forwards with a ball from the centre line and cross the ball for two central players to shoot or head at goal. All players rotate one place so that they now cross, finish or await their turn to do so. A few ball-retrievers, or spare players awaiting their turn, can be used to ensure that the ball supply is maintained.

Equipment: Six cones, two portable goals, a good supply of balls

Progressions: The coach can ask the crossers to practise a particular type of cross (e.g. out-swinging cross, near-post cross, hard-driven cross etc.).

drill 77

Purpose: Crossing a moving ball to the far post area and finishing the cross from that position

Practice set-up: A group of players organise themselves around a goal guarded by a goalkeeper. A server stands on the touchline with a supply of balls, faced by another player, the crosser, 10–15 yds away. A file of players stands at the other side of the goal. The drill proceeds with the server rolling a gentle pass for the facing player to cross. The first player in the file, the striker, breaks off and tries to finish with a shot or header. The players all rotate quickly.

Equipment: A good supply of balls

Progressions: The crosser moves to a wider position so that the cross becomes more difficult to perform.

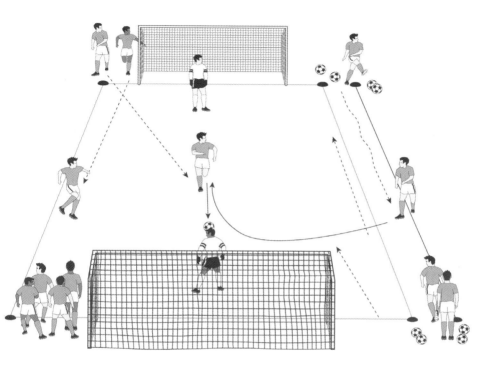

Purpose: Crossing on the run, and timing runs to head at goal

Practice set-up: Two portable goals are placed 15–20 yds apart, each with a goalkeeper. There are three files of players at both ends: two files of players act in pairs and stand to one side of a goal; the other file stands 15–20 yds away from the other side of the goal in a marked channel. The wider files of players have a good ball supply at both ends. The drill starts with one player running with the ball along the channel while a pair of players runs parallel and centrally, competing to receive his cross and to try and score. All players join their respective files at the other end and the drill continues in the opposite direction. The files should change over so that they both get crossing and finishing practice.

Equipment: Four cones, two portable goals, a good supply of balls

Progressions: The coach can ask the players to run with the ball a little faster to add an edge to their crossing techniques.

drill 79

Purpose: Low crosses and short, snap shots

Practice set-up: A goal defended by a goalkeeper is set up using posts. Two stand on both sides of the goal. One acts as a winger and stands in a wide position approx 10 yards from goal. Each winger has a good supply of balls. The first winger from one side runs down the flank and crosses the ball on the move along the ground, for the striker to move in and look to score in one touch of the ball. As soon as this is completed, the same move is carried out by the two players on the other side of the goal as the goalkeeper turns to deal with the situation. After a set number of repetitions the wingers and strikers change roles.

Equipment: Two poles and 8–12 balls

Progressions: Change the sides that the wingers cross the ball from so that they need to use both right and left foot.

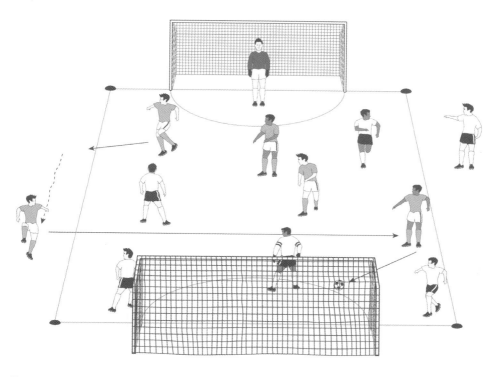

Purpose: Selecting where to cross the ball and finishing while under challenge from opponents

Practice set-up: On an area measuring 20 yds long by 30 yds wide, two teams play 4 vs 5 or 5 vs 5 with two portable goals, each defended by a goalkeeper. Two wingers, one on each side of the field, stand outside the area. Two teams of players play normal football and when the attacking team gets near a goal, they pass the ball to either of the wingers. The winger receiving the ball must try to cross the ball for another player on the same team, who attempts to score from the cross. Play restarts with the other team having possession and playing the other way.

Equipment: Four cones, two portable goals, one or two balls, coloured bibs

Progressions: The coach can count the number of crosses in the game, or the number of goals scored, and award points to the team that has amassed the highest total.

GOALKEEPING

All youngsters should experience this specialist position, which is so unlike any other in the team. As the only player who can use his hands to stop the ball, many of the skills and techniques the goalkeeper needs to learn differ greatly from those needed by outfield players. The goalkeeper has a special responsibility in the team as the 'last line of defence' and can help his team win by making match-winning saves. The goalkeeper not only needs to become a good 'shot-stopper' and deal with crosses, he also is the 'first line of attack' in his team and needs to know how to throw and kick the ball accurately to start off attacking moves for his team. The drills provided are geared to the specifics of goalkeeping and they will give would-be goalkeepers practice in the relevant skills of the position. It is important that youngsters all get some experience in this position and don't specialise too soon. Players who have only played outfield positions can find playing in goal a lot of fun and something they are good at.

Manchester United's goalkeeper, Edwin Van der Sar, demonstrates the bravery needed by goalkeepers when making this last-ditch save against Chelsea's Florent Malovda. (Photo: Adam Davy)

Purpose: Correct diving techniques

Practice set-up: The goalkeeper lies on his side along the ground, with his chest facing the coach. The coach rolls the ball along the ground to one side of the goalkeeper. The goalkeeper pushes along the ground to catch or direct the ball away. He then returns to his position and repeats the action. The coach should repeat the exercise a set number of times, but should take care not to exhaust the goalkeeper. (Repetitions of 6–10 may be appropriate.)

Equipment: A good supply of balls

Progressions: Gradually extend the goalkeeper's skills by rolling the ball a little further from him, or by rolling it a little faster, so that his technique is put under continual but controlled pressure.

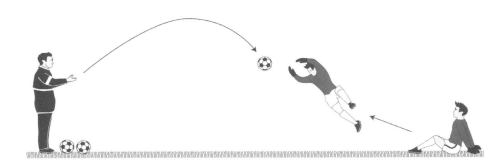

drill 82

Purpose: Recovery and diving technique

Practice set-up: The goalkeeper sits on the ground faced by the coach who has a ball in his hands. The coach serves the ball to the side of the goalkeeper, who dives sideways to catch it and return it to the coach for the next service. The coach serves the ball six times to the right side and then six times to the left side.

Equipment: A good supply of balls

Progressions: The coach should gradually extend the goalkeeper by throwing the ball a little higher or further from him and alternately left and right as the session progresses.

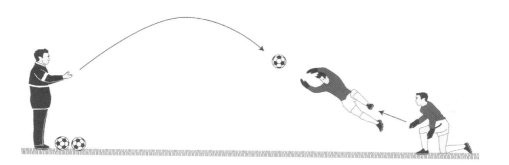

Purpose: Correct diving technique

Practice set-up: The goalkeeper kneels on one knee and faces the coach, who holds a ball. The coach proceeds to toss the ball to one side of the goalkeeper, who dives to catch it and return it to the coach. (Note: the toss should be to the side where the knee is off the ground.) The coach should ensure that the goalkeeper is diving along the side of his body, so that he can see the ball clearly and use the softer part of his body to land.

Equipment: A good supply of balls

Progressions: Gradually extend the goalkeeper by serving the ball faster or further from his body so that he needs to react more quickly or improve his diving techniques.

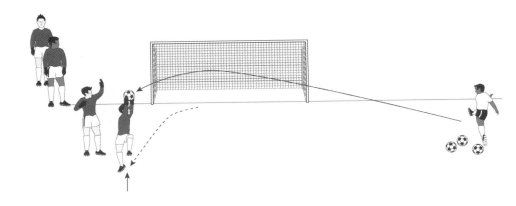

Purpose: Catching the ball from a cross

Practice set-up: A file of goalkeepers faces the coach, who stands to the side 20–25 yds away. The coach serves a high, looping throw for each goalkeeper in turn. Each goalkeeper must move and jump to catch the ball as high in its flight as possible before returning it to the coach and going to the back of the file. The goalkeeper needs to be aware of his timing and should try to come a little late so that he gathers momentum and arrives to take the ball in a forward direction.

Equipment: A good supply of balls

Progressions: The coach can stand further away and either use a javelin service or kick the ball from his hands. This increases the difficulty for the goalkeeper, who has to assess the flight of the ball and catch it at the top of his jump.

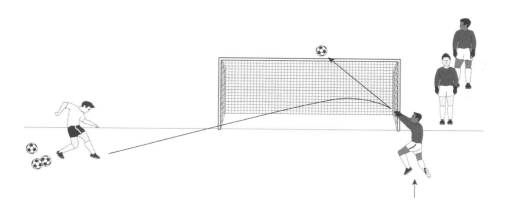

Purpose: Punching the ball from a cross. Learning to assess the ball flight and technique.

Practice set-up: A file of goalkeepers stands in front of and to one side of the goal. The coach, who has a good supply of balls, stands on the other side of the goal and further back. The coach serves a ball to each goalkeeper and they take turns to punch the ball high and far away from the goal, using either one hand or both. (Note: ensure children use a safe technique and wear goalkeeper gloves.) The coach should make sure that young goalkeepers watch the ball's flight carefully and punch right through the bottom part of it so that the ball travels far and high out of the danger area.

Equipment: A good supply of balls

Progressions: The coach stands at various positions on the flank and delivers a more realistic and difficult service for the goalkeeper to deal with.

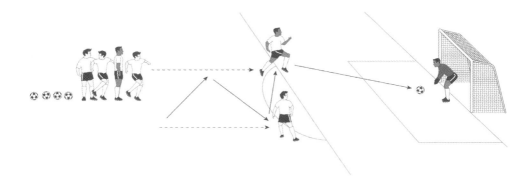

Purpose: Positioning and shot-stopping

Practice set-up: Two players pass the ball between them in a channel 12–18 yds wide in front of the goalkeeper. They pass quickly and shoot within 1–3 passes. The goalkeeper gets practice in changing his angle and position to face each shot. A supply of balls keeps the practice flowing and the coach should ensure that the pair of players continually attack the goal, thus keeping the goalkeeper under pressure. The goalkeepers should change every three or four minutes so they can recover.

Equipment: A good supply of balls, six cones

Progressions: The coach can encourage the players shooting at goal to try and use as many varied techniques as possible to give the goalkeeper more realistic practice in positioning and stopping their shots.

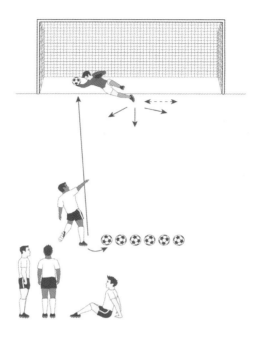

Purpose: Practising quick reactions, positioning and shot-stopping

Practice set-up: One or two players stand behind 6–8 footballs, positioned 15–20 yds from the goal. The goalkeeper stands off his goal line. The player starts at the end ball and shoots in sequence as the goalkeeper reacts quickly to save each shot. The next player lines up the balls and shoots starting from the other side, moving to hit each ball in sequence until he has fired all six to eight shots at goal.

Equipment: Six to eight balls

Progressions: The player shooting at goal can strike any ball at random so that the goalkeeper has little time to react and has to move his feet and take the correct angle for the different shots. Thus he will need to make the best out of every situation in order to protect his goal.

Purpose: Correct diving technique

Practice set-up: A file of goalkeepers stands in the centre of the goal with a ball each in their arms. One at a time, they jog with the ball towards the coach, who stands in front in the penalty area. The coach points to the left or right and the goal-keeper dives with the ball while on the move, rolling over and recovering with the ball still in his hands. He then returns to the back of the file, awaiting his turn to repeat the action.

Equipment: A good supply of balls

Progressions: The coach can encourage the goalkeepers to dive a little higher and help them to land more effectively by getting their body into a comfortable shape and relaxing the muscles not actually used in the action.

drill 89

Purpose: To gather a ball rolling along the ground

Practice set-up: The goalkeepers stand in a file facing the coach, who is 6–10 yds away. The coach serves the ball, with his feet or hands, along the ground for the first player to come forwards and gather the ball. The goalkeeper then uses a bowling action to roll the ball back to the coach before quickly returning to the end of the file. In this way, each goalkeeper receives fielding practice.

Equipment: One ball

Progressions: The coach can ask players to speed up play, or can roll the ball to the sides of the goalkeepers so that they have to employ better footwork.

Goalkeeping **115**

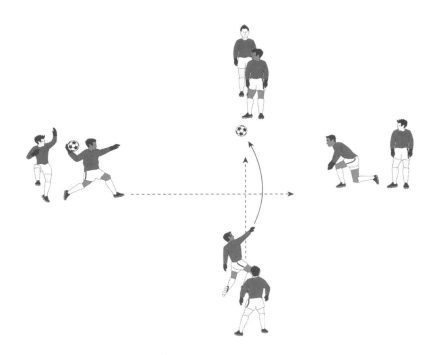

Purpose: To catch a hard-driven ball at chest level

Practice set-up: Four files of players stand 10–15 yds apart in a cross formation. Two leading players on adjacent files hold a ball in their hands. The players throw the balls forcefully towards the chests of the players opposite, who catch them and throw them back to the next players in the files. After throwing the ball, players join the end of the file to await their turn.

Equipment: Two balls (a few spare balls should also be available)

Progressions: Speed up play or serve the ball to the sides of the player (though not too far away) to incorporate better footwork and catching practice.

Purpose: Fielding a ball rolling along the ground

Practice set-up: The players stand in pairs, 3–8 yds apart. One holds the ball and faces his partner. Two lines are marked on the ground behind them to show the practice area. (Alternatively, cones can be used.) The player with the ball dribbles it along the ground, slowly driving the other player, the goalkeeper, backwards. The goalkeeper either controls the ball with his feet or gathers it with his hands and returns it quickly to the oncoming player until they reach the line. They then reverse roles and direction until they reach the opposite line and then repeat the drill.

Equipment: Two cones, one ball

Progressions: Speed up play or use various fielding techniques, such as going down on one knee, or keeping the feet together and a straight back to cup and scoop the ball up into the goalkeeper's arms from the ground.

drill 92

Purpose: Positioning and shot-stopping

Practice set-up: A portable goal, defended by a goalkeeper, is erected using two cones, and a pair of players stands 15–20 yds away on both sides of the goal. One ball is shared between all the players. The players are allowed a maximum of three passes before shooting from behind the line. If the goalkeeper saves, he rolls the ball to the other pair; if the shot goes past him, he turns quickly to face a shot from the other side. In this way, the practice alternates from end to end.

Equipment: Six cones, one ball (keep a spare ball handy)

Progressions: The coach can ask the players to hit a specific type of shot (e.g. high in the corner or low and hard at the goalkeeper's body), thus giving the goalkeeper more realistic practice.

Purpose: Quick reactions, agility and shot-stopping technique

Practice set-up: The goalkeeper stands on a soft surface facing a wall or shooting board 3–6 yds away. The coach, or a player, stands behind and slightly to the side of the goalkeeper and serves the ball by hand or foot so that it rebounds from the wall. The goalkeeper sees the ball coming late and has to react or dive quickly to catch it. He rolls it back to the coach and gets ready for the next service.

Equipment: One or two balls, a rebound surface

Progressions: The coach can feed the ball a little harder or wider, or the goal-keeper can move a little closer to the wall so that there is less time for him to react to the oncoming ball.

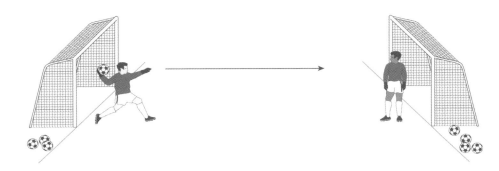

Purpose: Various shot-stopping situations and throwing the ball

Practice set-up: Two portable goals (preferably with nets) are erected 10–20 yds apart, and are defended by two goalkeepers who have a good supply of balls. Each goalkeeper tosses the ball, in turn, from just in front of their own goal line, trying to score in the other goal. The other goalkeeper tries to save the ball and, in turn, throws the ball towards the far goal, and so the drill continues.

Equipment: Two portable goals, a good supply of balls

Progressions: The goalkeepers can throw the ball harder to give each other better quality practice, or the coach can ask them to serve the ball in a particular way (e.g. low or lobbing the ball under the crossbar) to give them practice at handling specific shots.

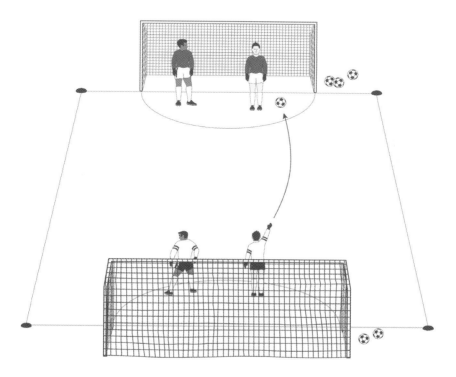

Purpose: Angling, positioning, shot-stopping and distribution

Practice set-up: Two portable goals (preferably with nets) are erected 10–20 yds apart, and each is defended by a pair of goalkeepers, who have a good supply of balls. One goalkeeper throws or kicks the ball towards the opposite goal to try and score. The goalkeepers take up appropriate positions to save the ball each time, and take turns to shoot at goal.

Equipment: Two portable goals, a good supply of balls

Progressions: The goalkeepers can strike the ball at goal much more aggressively. This not only gives their opponents valuable practice, but also improves their own kicking techniques, which all good goalkeepers require in the modern game.

WARMING DOWN

The drills that are always done at the conclusion of the coaching session are used to help the players, who have been working hard physically and mentally, to return the body and mind to its normal state. This period should always be entertaining for young players so that they will want to come back for more, which is why small groups, light-hearted activities and competition are used. The main function is not the development of skills, although obvious errors can be quickly pointed out, but to finish the session in a gradual fashion and to have some fun and social interaction in the process. The coach can also use this to help reinforce the young players' learning by getting them to positively think and visualise the skills and techniques they have been practising. This will assist their memory and it will be easier for them to recall and use the skills next time.

Peter Cech, the Chelsea goalkeeper shown here during a training session, has become one of the best players in his position in the world. Like all great players he prepares well by always having a methodical 'warm-down' after matches and training sessions. (Photo: Daniel Hambury)

drill 96

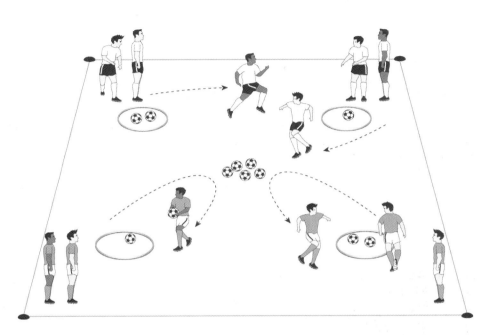

Purpose: For fun, competition and to return the body to its normal state

Practice set-up: Four files of players stand behind four hoops 10–20 yds apart. Twelve balls are placed in the centre. One player from each team runs to collect a ball in his arms and carries it back to place it in his hoop. The drill continues until one player has four balls in their hoop. During the drill, each player is allowed to go and steal a ball for his hoop from another player's hoop instead of from the centre, if it is advantageous for his team. The next player from the team goes until they all have a chance.

Equipment: Four hoops, twelve balls

Progressions: Add more balls. Count the team scores.

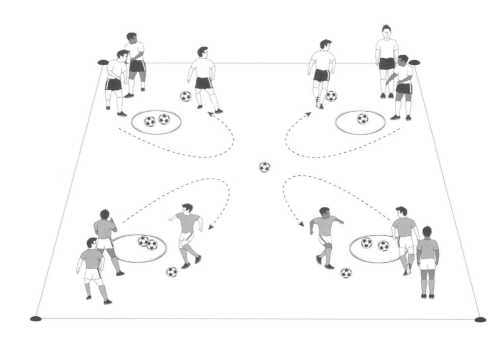

Purpose: For fun, competition and to return the body to its normal state

Practice set-up: Four files of players stand behind four hoops as in drill 96, and aim to get four balls inside their hoop to win. However, instead of using their hands to carry the balls, they must dribble the ball. The same rules as in drill 96 apply. Players are not allowed to kick other balls as they practise. However, as before, they can steal another ball by dribbling it from another hoop back into their own.

Equipment: Four hoops, twelve balls

Progressions: Add more balls.

drill 98

Purpose: Light running, competition and some flexibility work

Practice set-up: Teams compete against each other in files of players who face a cone 10–12 yds away. The front player has a ball under his arm and he proceeds to run around the cone and back to his file. He turns his back and passes the ball over his head for the rest of the file to do likewise until the ball reaches the back player, who receives the ball and repeats the drill. Each player in turn runs with the ball and passes it overhead along the team for a set number of repetitions, which is decided by the coach.

Equipment: One cone and one ball per team

Progressions: The players can perform different movements as they run to and from the file of players (e.g. side skips, running backwards, forward rolls).

Purpose: Fun, competition and helping the body to recover

Practice set-up: Teams line up in files facing a marker 10–20 yds away. The front player has a ball at his feet and proceeds to run with it at speed around the marker. He then returns to his file, where the remaining players stand with their legs wide apart to make a tunnel. The player passes the ball through the tunnel so that the back player stops it and proceeds to run with it around the marker. The coach sets a number of repetitions for each team.

Equipment: One cone and one ball per team

Progressions: The coach can ask each player to use different skills when running with the ball (e.g. left foot only, alternate feet, or having a player complete a full circle with the ball around the cone before returning with it to his team).

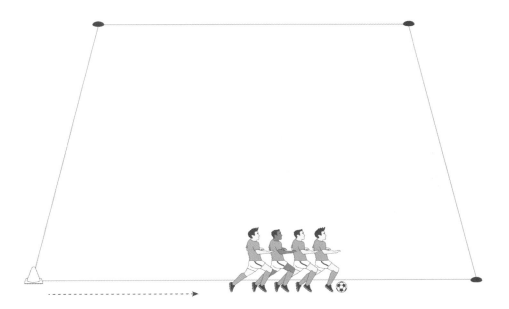

Purpose: Fun and warming down activity

Practice set-up: Files of players form a chain by each one holding the bottom of another's training bib or shirt at the back. The first player in the chain has a ball at his feet and, on a diamond shape 10 yds wide at each marker, he proceeds to run with the ball, keeping it under control just in front of himself as the chain moves in unison with him around the diamond. When they reach the starting point again, the first player goes to the back and the exercise is repeated. The chain must not break, otherwise the players must start again.

Equipment: Four cones, one set of coloured bibs, one ball

Progressions: A heavier medicine ball can be used, or the players can be told to move in both directions around the square. (Ensure the drill is carried out safely and bibs are not held too tight or players move too fast.)

drill 101

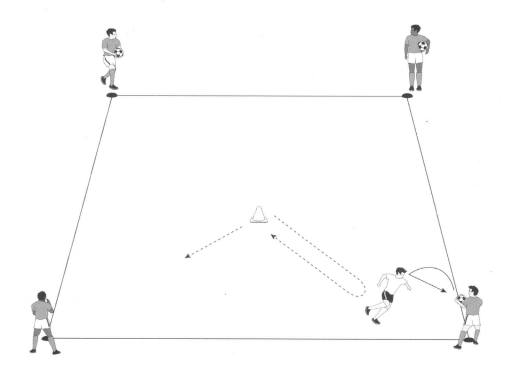

Purpose: Heading and general warming down

Practice set-up: Four players, each holding a ball in their hands, stand beside a cone in a 10–15 yd square. One player stands beside a cone placed in the centre. The central player runs to each of the other players to receive a gentle underarm throw in the centre which he must head back for each player to catch. After each header, the player has to touch the centre cone before moving clockwise around the square. He performs a second circuit, but during the second circuit he runs around the back of each player that he heads the ball to each time, so that he finally completes eight headers in all.

Equipment: Five cones, four balls

Progressions: The central player, if the coach wishes, can be asked to perform various skills, such as passing from the ground, volleying the ball or controlling the ball before he passes.